How Many Birds?

by Don L. Curry

Consultant:

Johanna Kaufman, Math Learning/
Resource Coordinator of the Dalton School

Books

Capstone Curriculum Publishing
Mankato, Minnesota

Adélie penguins

Look at these penguins waddling across the ice. Can you think of a quick way to count them?

1 2 3 4 5

6 7 8 9 10

We can count them quickly if we put them into groups. Are you ready? Let's count.

2

I see one group of two puffins sitting on a rock. How many puffins are in that one group?

1   2   3   4   5

One group of two puffins equals two puffins.

If you write it as a math problem, it will look like this:

 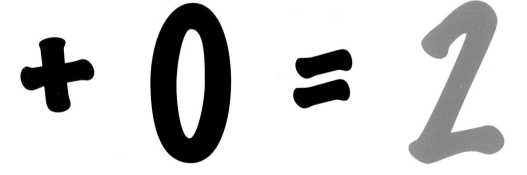

4

white pelicans

Now, I see two groups of two pelicans standing in a pond. How many pelicans are in the pond?

Two groups of two pelicans equal four pelicans.

1 2 3 **4** 5

4

If you write it as a math problem, it will look like this:

2 + 2 = 4

6

I see three groups of two flamingos standing in a swamp. How many flamingos are in the three groups?

1   2   3   4   5

Three groups of two flamingos equal six flamingos.

6

If you write it as a math problem, it will look like this:

$$2 + 2 + 2 = 6$$

8

I see four groups of two royal terns on the beach. How many royal terns are in the four groups? Four groups of two royal terns equal eight royal terns on the beach.

1   2   3   4   5

If you write it as a math problem, it will look like this:

$$2 + 2 + 2 + 2 = 8$$

10

bald eagles

Wow! Look at all of the bald eagles. Can you count them all?

Five groups of two bald eagles equal ten bald eagles perched on a branch.

1   2   3   4   5

If you write it as a math problem,
it will look like this:

$$2 + 2 + 2 + 2 + 2 = 10$$

6   7   8   9   **10**

3

blue titmice

Another quick way to count is to use groups of three. Here is one group of three young blue titmice crying for food.

1 2 **3** 4 5

One group of three blue titmice equals three young blue titmice.

If you write it as a math problem, it will look like this:

 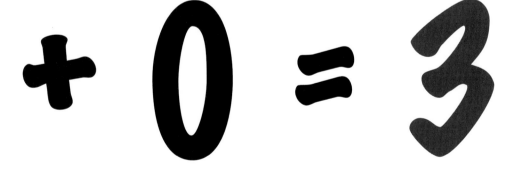

6

Look at the swans swimming in the pond. How many swans do you count?

1   2   3   4   5

Two groups of three swans equal
six swimming swans.

6

If you write it as a
math problem, it
will look like this:

3 + 3 = 6

9

fulvous whistling ducks

Look! See the whistling ducks? There are three groups of three whistling ducks wading in the marsh. How many whistling ducks do you count?

1   2   3   4   5

Three groups of three whistling ducks equal nine whistling ducks wading in the marsh.

9

If you write it as a math problem, it will look like this:

$$3 + 3 + 3 = 9$$

How many birds?

Count the groups of two. You tell me how many birds you see!

$2 + 0 = 2$

$2 + 2 = 4$

$2 + 2 + 2 = 6$

1   2   3   4   5

$2 + 2 + 2 + 2 = 8$

$2 + 2 + 2 + 2 + 2 = 10$

1 **2** **3** **4** **5**

$3 + 0 = 3$

Now how many birds do you see?

Count each kind of bird using groups of three.

$3 + 3 = 6$

$3 + 3 + 3 = 9$

6   7   8   9   10

Adélie penguins

Remember all of these penguins waddling across the ice? Now you know an easy way to count them.

1　　2　　3　　4　　5

How many groups of penguins are on the ice? How many penguins are in each group?

If you write it as a math problem, it will look like this:

2 + 2 + 2 + 2 = 8

Note To Teachers and Parents

How Many Birds? opens to children the world of birds while building skip-counting skills. The combination of full-color photographs and mathematical facts, as well as locational and bird-specific vocabulary, and a glossary filled with facts about birds makes this book an excellent cross-curricular teaching tool.

The real-life photographs, new vocabulary, and bird facts encourage lively discussions that build oral language skills and extend science concepts, while developing skip-counting skills. In addition, the list of Internet sites, the bibliography, and hands-on projects bring this book's information to learners of all styles.

Hands-On Projects

My Bird-Counting Book

Materials:
- 11" x 14" sheets of paper
- crayons
- old magazines

Invite children to create their own skip-counting books. Set up a booklet by folding a stack of 11" x 14" sheets of paper in half and stapling them together at the fold. Invite children to write 2 on the outside upper corner of the first page. Have them continue on to the next page with 4, then 6, and so on up to 10, or even higher if you wish. Remind children that a book has a cover where they write the title of the book and the name of the author and illustrator. Once the books have a cover and counting pages, invite children to use their drawings or photographs from magazines and Internet sites to illustrate the number on each page. When children have completed the illustrations, challenge them to write an addition number sentence detailing how to get to the number displayed on the page using a mathematical equation ($2 + 2 + 2 + 2 = 8$).

Once they finish the counting by 2s book, have them create a counting by 3s version using the same layout but starting with 3 and ending with 9, or higher for those who need the challenge. Consider having children add a sentence or two sharing information about the birds they use to illustrate the counting skill. Have *How Many Birds?* on display for children to refer to as they work. Display children's books for others to read and enjoy.

Experiment with Gliding

Materials: sheets of lightweight paper (8½" x 11")

Explanation: Discuss with children that many birds, like the bald eagle, ride on the air when they are flying. Riding on the air is called gliding. The bird will flap its wings to take off and get going, but once it is up in the sky, it will sometimes ride on the air by keeping its wings extended outward. Some birds can travel many miles without flapping their wings. Invite children to conduct the experiment below to learn more about gliding.

Steps to Follow:

Step 1. Take a flat piece of paper and hold it in the air at shoulder height. Let the sheet of paper drop. Have children watch and then explain what happens as the paper falls to the ground.

Step 2. Now crinkle the same piece of paper into a ball. Hold the sheet of paper at the same height you held the flat paper and then let it drop. Have children explain what happens to the crinkled paper and how it behaved differently than when it was flat.

Step 3. Provide pairs of children with two sheets of paper. Have one partner crinkle the sheet of paper while the other child keeps the sheet of paper flat. Invite the partners to drop the flat and the crinkled pieces of paper at the same time. Have children explain the difference between how the two pieces of paper fell. Have them take special note of the speed at which each paper drops and the way in which each descends to the floor.

Discussion: What happened to the crinkled sheet of paper when it was dropped? What happened to the flat sheet of paper when it was dropped? Imagine a bird with its wings folded into its sides. Which piece of paper is it most like? Imagine a bird with its wings fully spread open. Which piece of paper is it most like? The flat sheet of paper is able to ride on the air much like the bird with its wings spread. If you take that flat sheet of paper outside on a windy day, you will really see how well it rides on the air. The crinkled sheet of paper is much like the bird with its wings tucked into its sides. A bird with its wings tucked away will fall to the ground much like the crinkled paper.

Internet Sites

Animal Bytes Puffin's Page

http://www.seaworld.org/animal_bytes/puffinsab.html

Homework Central

http://www.homeworkcentral.com

The Life of Birds

http://www.pbs.org/lifeofbirds

Science for Kids

http://www.ars.usda.gov/is/kids/

Smithsonian Magazine's Kid's Castle

http://www.kidscastle.si.edu/

Song Birds

http://www.math.sunysb.edu/~tony/birds/

What Makes Birds Fly?

http://wings.ucdavis.edu/Book/Animals/intermediate/birds-01.html

The World of Penguins

http://www.pbs.org/wnet/nature/penguins/

Zoom Birds

http://www.EnchantedLearning.com/subjects/birds/

Books About Birds

Bailey, Jill and David Burnie. *Eyewitness Explorers: Birds.* New York: DK Publishing, 1999.

Brownlie, Betty. *The Life Cycle of the Royal Albatross.* Auckland, New Zealand: Ashton/Scholastic, 1995

Burnie, David. *Eyewitness Books: Birds.* New York: Alfred A. Knopf, 1988.

Cowcher, Helen. *Antarctica.* New York: Farrar, Straus and Giroux, 1990

Hirschi, Ron. *What Is a Bird?* New York: Walker and Company, 1987

Lang, Aubrey. *Eagles: Sierra Club Wildlife Library.* Boston: Little, Brown and Company, 1990.

Parsons, Alexandra. *Amazing Birds.* New York: Alfred A. Knopf, 1990

Wallace, Karen. *A Day at Seagull Beach.* New York: DK Publishing, 1999.

Yolen, Jane. *Owl Moon.* New York: Putnam, 1987

Glossary

Adélie Penguin

- Adélie penguins are a part of the *Spheniscidae* family and of the order of *Sphenisciformes*. There are six species of penguin. The scientific name of the Adélie penguin is *Pygoscelis adeliae*.

- Adélie penguins are seabirds that stand straight up with their feet flat on the ground. They weigh about 11 lbs. (5 kg) and can grow to be 28 in. (71 cm) tall. The penguin's ancestors could fly. Penguins today are excellent swimmers and divers but cannot fly. Adélie penguins can swim at speeds of more than 25 mph (40 kph).

- Adélie penguins live in the Antarctic. Adélie penguins usually nest away from the coastline, and since they cannot walk well on their short legs, they often sled over the ice on their stomachs.

Horned Puffin

- Horned puffins are seabirds that belong to the *Alcidae* family, which includes auks, auklets, murres, murrelets, and guillemots. They belong to the order of *Charadriiformes*. The scientific name of the horned puffin is *Fratercula corniculata*.

- Horned puffins can grow to be about 14 in. (36 cm) long and weigh about 1.25 lbs. (600 g). They have fat bodies, short wings, and orange or red webbed feet which are far back on their body. Horned puffin's bodies are built more for swimming than for flying. They swim underwater using their wings to move and their webbed feet for steering.

- Horned puffins spend the winter far offshore in the Northern Pacific Ocean and only visit land to breed in the summer. In Alaska, horned puffins breed on coastal islands and headlands.

White Pelican

- White pelicans are seabirds that belong to the *Pelecanidae* family and the order *Pelecaniformes*. The species name for the white pelican is *Pelecanus erythrorhynchos*. There are six species of pelican.

- White pelicans can grow to be 70 in. (180 cm) long, with a wing span as wide as 9 ft. (2.7 meters), and can weigh up to 30 lbs. (14 kg). White pelicans are large-bodied, short-legged, and have bills that are longer than their heads with a pouch of skin attached to the lower mandible (jaw) which holds the food they catch. The pouch holds more food than the pelican's stomach, about 3 gal. (11 *l*) when full.

- White pelicans are found from British Columbia south to northern California during breeding season. Wintering grounds are from California, the Gulf Coast, and Florida south to Panama. They prefer shallow lakes and coastal lagoons.

Lesser Flamingo

- Lesser flamingos belong to the *Phoenicopteridae* family and the order *Ciconiiformes*. The species name for the lesser flamingo is *Phoeniconaias minor*.

- Lesser flamingos stand about 40 in. (101 cm) tall with long stilt-like legs, deep pink feathers, webbed feet, and a curved bill and neck. The bird's neck curves, looking very much like a letter *S*. Its head is small and its beak is flat and downward curved. The flamingo flies with its neck and legs outstretched. Flamingos get their pink color from the food they eat. The lesser flamingo feeds on blue-green algae by filtering water through the laminea (tiny hair-like filters) in its beak.

- The majority of the lesser flamingo populations are found in large, shallow lakes in east and central Africa, but large populations are also found in Pakistan and India.

Royal Tern

- Royal terns belong to the *Laridae* family and the order *Charadriiformes*. The species name for royal terns is *Sterna maxima*.

- Royal terns can grow to 20 in. (51 cm) long from the tip of their yellow bill to the end of their forked tail. They may grow to have a wingspan as wide as 45 in. (114 cm) from tip to tip.

- Royal terns breed from the Caribbean north to Maryland, as well as western Mexico and western Africa. Royal terns nest on islands and barrier beaches.

Bald Eagle

- Bald eagles belong to the *Accipitridae* family and the order *Falconiformes*. The species name for bald eagles is *Haliaeetus leucocephalus*. Bald eagles are related to vultures, hawks, and falcons.

- Bald eagles are birds of prey. The bald eagle has white feathers on the head, tail, and neck, while the body is brown. Males can grow to be as large as 34 in. (86 cm) long, while females can be as long as 37 in. (93 cm). The wingspan of a male can grow to be as wide as 85 in. (216 cm), while the female can grow up to 90 in. (229 cm).

- Bald eagles range over most of the North American continent, from Alaska and Canada to northern Mexico. In the United States, there are an estimated 50,000 bald eagles, with 80 percent of them found in Alaska.

Blue Titmouse

- Blue titmice belong to the *Paridae* family and the order *Passeriformes*. The species name for blue titmice is *Parus caeruleus*.

- Blue titmice are about 4 in. (11 cm) long. Adults have green-blue upper bodies with a single white bar on the wings and yellow undersides. Blue titmice usually lay seven or eight eggs; it usually takes two weeks to do so. The eggs of the blue titmouse will weigh more than the female who laid them.

- Blue titmice can be found throughout most of Europe and into Siberian Asia. Their habitats are mixed woods, hedges, and gardens.

Mute Swan

- Mute swans belong to the *Anatidae* family along with all ducks, geese, and swans. Mute swans are members of the subfamily *Cygninae* that includes all swans. Mute swans belong to the order *Anseriformes*. The species name for mute swans is *Cygnus olor.*

- Mute swans may grow to 5 ft. (152 cm) long, weigh as much as 30 lbs. (13.6 kgs), and have a wingspan that reaches 7 ft. (3.5 m) across. Mute swans have white plumage (feathers), black legs, and an orange-red bill with a black knob near their eyes. Young swans are called cygnets, the adult male is called a cob, and the adult female is called a pen.

- Mute swans are native to Europe and Asia and were introduced into the United States, where large populations now inhabit the Atlantic coastal states from Connecticut to Virginia as well as several mid-western states.

Fulvous Whistling Duck

- Fulvous whistling ducks belong to the *Anatidae* family along with all ducks, geese, and swans. Fulvous whistling ducks belong to the order *Anseriformes*. The species name for fulvous whistling ducks is *Dendrocygna bicolor.*

- Fulvous whistling ducks have a wingspan that can grow to 9 in. (22 cm), and weigh as much as 2 lbs. (850 g). Fulvous whistling ducks make a whistling sound that is harsh and high-pitched. They are active day and night. Fulvous whistling ducks are omnivorous (they will eat both plants and animals). Fulvous whistling ducks eat grains, water plants, snails, and invertebrates (creatures without a backbone).

- Fulvous whistling ducks are found in Trinidad and Tobago, South America, Southern United States, and Africa. The fulvous whistling duck is found on flat, open land areas, primarily in swamps or marshes.

Index

A+ Books are published by Capstone Press
P.O. Box 669, Mankato, Minnesota 56002
http://www.capstone-press.com

EDITORIAL CREDITS:

Susan Evento, Managing Editor/Product Development; Don L. Curry, Senior Editor; Jannike Hess, Designer; Kimberly Danger and Heidi Schoof, Photo Researchers; Content Consultant: Johanna Kaufman

LIBRARY OF CONGRESS CATALOGING-IN-PUBLICATION DATA:

Don L. Curry
    How Many Birds?/by Don L. Curry; consultant, Johanna Kaufman.
        p. cm.
    Includes bibliographical references and index.
    Summary: Simple text and photographs present a variety of birds for the reader to count and add.
    ISBN 0-7368-7039-3 (Hard)   ISBN 0-7368-7052-0 (Paper)
    1. Addition—Juvenile literature. 2. Counting—Juvenile literature. 3. Birds—Juvenile literature. [1. Addition. 2. Counting. 3. Birds.] I. Kaufman, Johanna. II. Title.
QA115 .C89 1999
513.2'11—dc21
[[E]]   99-052182

PHOTO CREDITS:

Cover: Stoneridge Images; *Title Page:* J.C. Carton/Bruce Coleman Inc.; *Pages 2–3, 24–25:* Index Stock Photography; *Pages 4–5, 20:* Index Stock Photography; *Pages 6, 20:* R.E. Barber; *Pages 8–9, 20:* Tom & Pat Leeson; *Pages 10–11, 21:* Rob & Ann Simpson; *Pages 12–13, 22:* Lynn M. Stone/Bruce Coleman Inc.; *Pages 14–15, 23:* R. Maler/Bruce Coleman Inc.; *Page 16–17, 23:* Norman Tomalin/Bruce Coleman Inc.; *Page 18–19, 23:* Michael P. Turco.